The Families of Perkins, Fairfield and King

SAN FRANCISCO

THE MURDOCK PRESS

1907

Published by
N. P. Maling
Sea Genes Family History & Genealogy Research
Seattle, Washington, United States
npmaling@gmail.com

The following monographs on the Perkins, Fairfield, and King families have been compiled after thorough research among the early probate and land records of Maine, New Hampshire, and Massachusetts, and the records of vital statistics of various towns. Numerous genealogical and historical publications have also been consulted, and citations to the authorities examined are freely given.

WILLIAM MORRELL EMERY,

Compiler.

Fall River Mass., April, 1907.

CONTENTS

PERKINS FAMILY

Perkins Family

The name of Perkins was not an uncommon one in the early history of New England. Among the heads of families bearing that name were the following:

§ Thomas and William, of Dover, N. H.

§ John, of Boston and Ipswich, Mass.

§ Isaac, of Ipswich.

§ Rev. William, of Boston, Weymouth, Ipswich, Gloucester, and Topsfield, Mass.

§ Abraham, of Hampton, N. H.

§ Edward, of Connecticut.

Thomas and William are believed to have been brothers, and it is undoubtedly from one of them that the Perkins family of Kennebunkport, Me., forming the subject of this monograph, descended. The other Kennebunkport line is from John of Ipswich, a genealogy of whose descendants has been published.

The name of William Perkins of Oyster River (now Durham), Dover, N. H., appears on the

Dover tax list of 1662. At a training, June 21, 1669, Will Perkins and Thomas Perkins took the oath of fidelity (Dover town records). Both were taxed in 1675, Thomas as of Dover Neck and Cocheco, and William as of Oyster River. That year William bought land in Exeter (New Hampshire deeds). Savage gives the probable date of Thomas Perkins's birth as 1628. In April, 1693, he deeded land to his son Nathaniel, of Dover (New Hampshire deeds). Says the *New England Historical and Genealogical Register* (vol. 10, p. 216): "There was a William Perkins at Dover, 1662-75, born, it is said, in the west of England, 1616, and died in Newmarket in 1732, aged 116." But in a deposition of record, dated March 1677-78, William Perkins says he was then aged about thirty-nine years—therefore born about 1639; and the New Hampshire probate records show that William Perkins died, intestate, at Newmarket in 1740, therefore probably about 101 years old at death. Newmarket was originally a part of Exeter.

As early as 1706 there was a Thomas Perkins in Greenland, N. H., then a part of Portsmouth, and lying near both Dover and Exeter, who bought land there that year, and in 1722 removed to Kennebunkport. He was probably born about 1675 (because one of his sons was born in 1700), and therefore could have been a son or grandson of Thomas or William of Dover. Because of the frequency of the name Thomas among the descendants of the Greenland Perkins, it is not unreasonable to conclude that he was a grandson of the Dover Thomas. His name is not found in published lists of the descendants of Abraham of Hampton.

For convenience, in the list given below, Thomas of Kennebunkport is regarded as the first generation.

Capt. THOMAS[1] PERKINS was for sixteen years a resident of Greenland, N. H. In February, 1705-06, he bought an estate there of fifty acres of marsh and meadow land, for one hundred pounds sterling, of Col. William Partridge, of Portsmouth, (New Hampshire deeds, vol. 5, p. 150) and resided thereon until 1722. In February of the latter year he sold out for four hundred and fifty pounds sterling to Thomas Parker, Esq., of Portsmouth, his wife Mary signing the deed (New Hampshire deeds, vol. 12, p. 420), and thereafter made his home in old Arundel, or Kennebunkport. The York deeds show that he had previously acquired considerable land there. He purchased of the heirs of William Reynolds all the land lying between Kennebunk River and a line running from Bass Cove through Great Pond to the sea (York

Deeds, vol. 10, p. 130, p. 268). "This land," says Bradbury's History of Kennebunkport, "having been mortgaged to Francis Johnson, of whom Stephen Harding purchased it, there was a contest for the possession of it. The dispute was submitted to arbitrators, who awarded fourteen fifteenths of the land to Capt. Perkins. This transaction caused a breach between the families, that a subsequent marriage did not wholly close."

Capt. Perkins erected a garrison house by Butler's Rocks. He was undoubtedly the Thomas Perkins who was a sentinel in Serg. Allison Brown's company of Indian fighters at Arundel, October 15, 1723, to June 12, 1724, and sergeant in Lieut. Brown's company, May 29 to November 19, 1725, (Massachusetts Muster Rolls, vol. 91, pp. 121, 125). His wife was Mary, daughter of John Banfield, of Portsmouth, (New Hampshire deeds, vol. 24, p. 45): Thomas Perkins of Arundel, and wife Mary to son John, of Boston coaster, their right in the estate of John Banfill, late of Portsmouth, said Mary being daughter of said Banfill, 1738; and said John Perkins sold the land 1738-39. Capt. Perkins died about 1741, says Bradbury. His children were born before he settled in Kennebunkport.

Children (Bradbury):

I. JOHN[2], m. Jane —; they gave a deed in 1727 (York deeds, vol. 12, p. 200); left no children, unless Zaccheus.

II. THOMAS, b. 1700; d. Feb. 22, 1752.

III. LEMUEL, m. Hannah Hutchins; he and his only child died of fever the same day.

IV. SAMUEL, m. Willie Bond; children— Samuel, Timothy, George, Thomas, John, Joseph, Alice.

V. GEORGE, d. 1736; his brother Thomas administered on his estate July 18, 1736; no descendants.

VI. ALVERSON.

VII. ZACCHEUS; he might have been John's son; no descendants.

VIII. MARY, m. George Murphy; no children.

IX. CHASEY, m. James Deshon; five children.

Capt. THOMAS[2] PERKINS (*Thomas[1]*), son of Capt. Thomas and Mary (Banfield) Perkins, was born in 1700, and died in Kennebunkport, February 22, 1752. Like his father, he was a property-owner and an influential citizen, and there was a tradition that he was King's surveyor. He commanded a company at the surrender of Louisburg to Sir William Pepperell in 1745 (*N. E. Hist. and Gen. Reg.*, vol. 22, p. 116), and was wrecked in going to Annapolis, Nova Scotia, in 1747 (Bradbury). From March 28, 1748, to June 7, 1749, he was captain of a company of sentinels on guard duty against the Indians at Arundel, some of his sons also serving in that company (Massachusetts Muster Rolls, vol. 92, p. 146, vol. 93, p. 1). He married Lydia Harding, daughter of Stephen Harding and Abigail (Littlefield) Harding, of Kennebunkport, who survived him. April 7, 1752, administration was granted to Abner Perkins on the estate of his father, Thomas Perkins, of Arundel, gentleman, (York Probate Records, vol. 8, p. 158).

Children (Bradbury):

I. ELIPHALET[3], b. 1724; d. 1776; m. Mary, daughter of Ensign Thomas and Mary (Wildes) Perkins. (See note, p. 25.)

II. ABNER, d. 1811; m. Sarah Robinson.

III. JOHN, m. Mehitable Goodwin, whose only child, Mehitable, m. Gen. John Lord, of Berwick.

IV. THOMAS, b. 1732; d. Nov. 8, 1820; m. Sarah, daughter of John and Sarah (Bayley) Baxter; a soldier in the French and Indian wars, and an ensign in the militia, 1771-72, (Muster Rolls). Children—Esther, Lydia, Thomas, Sarah, Mary, John.

V. GEORGE, m. Mary, daughter of Benjamin Meeds and Mary (March) Lord; removed to Wells; large family.

VI. Capt. JAMES PERKINS, d. Nov. 9, 1825; m. (1) Sarah, daughter of Rev. John Hovey; (2) 1797, Mrs. Hannah Coit, of Saco; during the Revolution, in 1776-77, he commanded a company in Col. John Frost's regiment, serving on the North River (Muster Rolls). Children—James, Ruth, Thomas, John, Joshua, Ebenezer, Lydia, Lucy, Joshua again, Tristram J., Mary.

VII. MARY, m. Samuel, son of Samuel and Anna (Andrews) Robinson, and brother of Sarah, above; five children.

ABNER[3] PERKINS (*Thomas[2]*, *Thomas[1]*), son of
Capt. Thomas and Lydia (Harding) Perkins,
was born in Kennebunkport, probably
between 1724 and 1730, and died there in
1811. He was engaged in farming. In 1748 he
served as scout in Capt. Jonathan Bean's
company, his name being borne on the rolls
from May 5 to November 24 (Muster Rolls, vol.
92, p. 164, vol. 93, p. 8). Then, until the
following June, he was corporal in the
company commanded by his father, and was
also clerk of the company (vol. 93, p. 1). In
1757 he was a member of Capt. John Fairfield's
Arundel company (vol. 95, p. 358). During the
Revolution he was a member of the town's
committee of safety for the year 1777. He
married Sarah Robinson, daughter of Samuel
and Anna (Andrews) Robinson, of Kennebunkport, her father having come from Rowley,
Mass., probably about 1730. She must have died
before April 30, 1802, because she is not named in
his will, executed on that date. He died in 1811,
his will being admitted to probate on June 17
(York probate records, vol. 23, p. 204).

Children (all mentioned in will):

I. DANIEL[4], m. (1) Dec. 4, 1777, Hannah, daughter of Jonathan, Jr., and Hannah (Griffin) Stone; (2) June 4, 1786, Eunice, daughter of Benjamin and Eunice (Lord) Thompson, of Kennebunkport.

II. ABNER, m. March 5, 1789, Mary daughter of Israel and Sarah (Perkins) Stone, of Kennebunkport.

III. JOTHAM, m. Olive Hill.

IV. STEPHEN, b. July 25, 1765; d. Aug. 31, 1833.

V. JACOB, m. Aug. 28, 1793, Elizabeth Hill, of Biddeford.

VI. ANNA, m. Oct 22, 1787, Benjamin, son of Jonathan, Jr., and Phebe (Downing) Stone, of Kennebunkport.

VII. SARAH, m. James P. Hill.

WILL OF ABNER PERKINS

IN THE NAME OF GOD, AMEN. I, Abner Perkins of Arundel in the county of York, yeoman, being weak in body, but of sound mind and memory, do this thirtieth day of April Anno Domini one thousand eight hundred and two, make and publish this my last will and testament in manner following, that is to say:

§ Imprimis. I give to my son Abner Perkins one acre of salt marsh lying on the Eastern branch in Batsson's River, adjoining Daniel Perkins's marsh.

§ Item. I give to my son Jacob Perkins my homestead farm with the buildings thereon, and all the rest of my real estate wherever it may be, to hold to him and his heirs and assigns forever, he paying to my children hereafter named, in one year after my decease, as follows:

§ To my son Abner Perkins, one hundred dollars.

§ To my son Daniel Perkins, five dollars.

§ To my son Stephen Perkins, five dollars.

§ To my son Jotham Perkins, twenty dollars.

§ To my two daughters Anna Stone and Sarah Hill, twenty dollars each.

And I do constitute and ordain my son Jacob Perkins sole executor to this my last will and testament. In testimony whereof I do hereunder set my hand and seal the day and year above written.

ABNER PERKINS. [Seal.]

§ Signed, sealed, published, pronounced, and declared by the said Abner Perkins as and for his last will and testament, who at his request and in his presence set our hands as witnesses to the same.

THOMAS PERKINS 3D.

JORDAN SMITH.

MILES RHOADES.

STEPHEN[4] PERKINS (*Abner*[3], *Thomas*[2], *Thomas*[1]), son of Abner and Sarah (Robinson) Perkins, was born in Kennebunkport, July 25, 1765, and died there August 31, 1833, (family records). He was engaged in farming. He married, April 22, 1790, Alice Stone, of Kennebunkport, born June 29, 1769, died January 14, 1850 (family records). She was the daughter of Col. Jonathan, Jr., and Phebe (Downing) Stone, and granddaughter of Jonathan and Hannah (Lovet) Stone, who came to Kennebunkport from Beverly about 1735. Two Perkins brothers and a sister married two sisters and a brother of this Stone family. Col. Stone served in the Revolution in 1778 (Muster Rolls).

Children (family records):

I. WILLIAM[5], b. July 15, 1791; d. Feb. 26, 1818; m. June, 1817, Mehitable Scammon Lord, who d. Jan. 29, 1818.

II. ANNA, b. April 8, 1793; d. Oct. 8, 1851; m. James A. Piper and Oliver Davis.

III. IVORY C., b. March 30, 1795.

IV. ALICE, b. Jan. 8, 1797; d. Jan. 1899; m. May, 1825, Nathaniel Snow, a merchant of Saco.

V. STEPHEN, b. Sept. 27, 1798; d. May 20, 1855.

VI. JONATHAN, b. April 11, 1800.

VII. SILAS, b. Feb. 16, 1803; d. Feb. 15, 1869; m. Eliza Foss.

VIII. PHEBE, b. March 31, 1805; d. 1879; m. John Chapman.

IX. CLEMENT, b. March 23, 1807; d. March 4, 1884.

X. ABNER, b. Jan. 18, 1810; d. April 27, 1891; m. Asenath Merrill.

CLEMENT[5] PERKINS (*Stephen*[4], *Abner*[3], *Thomas*[2], *Thomas*[1]), son of Stephen and Alice (Stone) Perkins, was born in Kennebunkport, March 23, 1807, and died there, March 4, 1884. Like numerous other young men of the town, he went to sea in early life and afterwards carried on a farm. He married, in 1837, Mrs. Lucinda (Fairfield) Emery, of Kennebunkport, daughter of Capt. William and Mary (King) Fairfield, who was born November 20, 1802, and died December 31, 1887. (See Fairfield family).

Children:

I. GEORGE CLEMENT[6], b. Aug. 23, 1839.

II. WILLIAM L., b. 1840; d. 1888; m. Mattie Moore; daughter, Lillie A.

III. ERNESTINE L., b. 1842; m. Henry M. Maling, of Portland; children—Alice H., Walter B., Ernest H., Lucy A.

IV. DAVID KING, b. 1843; d. Nov. 1893; m. Mary Sparks; children—Ernestine, G. Clement, Alma, Mabel, Walter M., Davida.

V. CAROLINE AMELIA, b. 1845.

GEORGE CLEMENT[6] PERKINS (*Clement*[5], *Stephen*[4], *Abner*[3], *Thomas*[2], *Thomas*[1]), son of Clement and Lucinda (Fairfield) Perkins, was born in Kennebunkport, August 23, 1839. He attended public school until his thirteenth year, when he shipped on board a sailing ship for New Orleans, and followed the calling of a sailor on ships engaged in the European trade. In 1855 he shipped "before the mast" on the sailing ship *Galatea* bound for San Francisco, where he arrived in the autumn of that year. Since that time he has been engaged in the business of merchandising, banking, farming, mining, whale fishery, and steamship transportation. In 1868 he was elected to the State Senate, serving eight years; has been president of the Merchants' Exchange in San Francisco; also of the San Francisco Art Association; is a director of the California Academy of Sciences and other public institutions. He is a member of the Commandery of California of the Military Order of the Loyal Legion of the United States, having been elected for services rendered during the Civil War. In 1875 he was elected Grand Master of the Grand Lodge of F. and A. M. of the State of California, having previously been elected and served on year each respectively as Deputy Grand Master, Senior Grand Warden, and Junior Grand Warden. He was elected Grand Commander of the Grand Commandery of Knights Templars of California in 1883, and the same year was elected Grand Junior Warden of the Grand Encampment of the Knights Templars, U.S.A. In 1879 he was elected Governor of California, serving until January, 1883; was appointed, July 24, 1893, United States Senator, to fill, until the election of his successor, the vacancy caused by the death of Hon. Leland Stanford, and took his seat August 8, 1893. In January, 1895, having made a thorough canvass before the people of his State, he was elected by the Legislature on the first ballot to fill the unexpired term. In the fall election of 1896 he was a candidate before the people of California for re-election, and received the indorsement of the Republican county conventions that comprised a majority of the senatorial and assembly districts in the State. When the Legislature convened in joint convention (January, 1897) for the purpose of electing a United States Senator, he was re-elected on the first ballot. In January, 1903, he was again re-elected on the first ballot for the term of six years, receiving every vote of the Republican members of the Legislature. His election was made unanimous on motion of a Democratic member of the Legislature. At the time of his election in 1897 and in 1903 he was absent from the State attending to his congressional duties in Washington. His term of service will expire March 3, 1909.

Mr. Perkins married at Marysville, Cal., May 3, 1864, Ruth Amelia Parker, who was born at Cork, Ireland, August 21, 1843, and christened in the Episcopal Church of that city when one year old. Her father, Edward Parker, was an English excise officer, and came to California with his wife and daughter when she was a child eight years of age. Mr. Parker died in Oroville in 1861, and his widow married William Hesse. She died, May 20, 1881, in San Francisco, naming George C. Perkins executor of her last will and Mrs. Perkins her sole legatee.

Children:

    I. FANNIE I., b. in Oroville, Cal., April 28, 1865; m. J. E. Adams.

    II. GEORGE E., b. in Oroville, Cal., May 6, 1867; m. Eva J. Quartman.

    III. SUSAN C., b. in Oroville, Cal., June 11, 1869; m. William H. Schmidt.

    IV. FRED K., b. in Oroville, Cal., Nov. 15, 1872.

    V. MILTON G., b. in San Francisco, May 27, 1876.

    VI. RUTH M., b. in San Francisco, Jan. 28, 1878.

    VII. GRACE PANSY, b. in Oakland, Cal., Oct. 12, 1882.

Perkins Note

Among several instances where the two Perkins families of Kennebunkport inter-married was that of Eliphalet[3], son of Capt. Thomas Perkins (see page 14), born 1724, died in Portland in 1776. He was a soldier in the old French War, and was probably at Louisburg with his father. He married

Mary[5] Perkins (*Thomas[4], Elisha[3], Thomas[2], John[1]*), daughter of Ensign Thomas and Mary (Wildes) Perkins, of Cape Porpoise (part of Kennebunkport). She was born in 1728, and died September 14, 1802. Her father came from Topsfield, Mass., and was the first of this line to settle in Kennebunkport. Their first American ancestor came to this country in 1630, and lived at Boston and Ipswich. Of this line was John[1], Thomas[2], Elisha[3], Thomas[4], Thomas[5], Abiel[6], who married, in 1794, Hugh McCulloch, of Scotch ancestry, (father of Hon. Hugh McCulloch (1808-1895), Secretary of the Treasury). Eliphalet and Mary Perkins had eight children—Ephraim, Eliphalet, Hannah, Lydia, Mary, Eunice, Lucy, and Eliphalet.

Eunice, born March 6, 1761, died August 10, 1834, married May 15, 1783, Isaac[5] Emery (*Jabez[4], Job[3], James[2], Anthony[1]*), of Kennebunk, descendant of Anthony Emery, who came to this country with his brother John in 1635. (See Fairfield family.) Isaac was born April 22, 1756 and died June 14, 1836. Their son, Capt. Isaac Emery, married Lucinda Fairfield (see Fairfield family), who married for her second husband Clement Perkins.

Two Thomas Perkinses came into Kennebunkport about the same time; both were men of property and influence; and each had a son, grandsons, and great grandsons of the same name, who at different times held the same offices. For these reasons it has been impossible to specify the office filled by each.

PERKINS ARMS

(from Perkins Genealogy, Essex Institute Collections, and Book of Family Crests)
Arms—Or, a fesse dancette, between ten billets ermines.
Crest—A pineapple proper, stalked and leaved vert.

FAIRFIELD FAMILY

FAIRFIELD FAMILY

There were two Fairfields in Massachusetts as early as 1638,—JOHN, variously of Charlestown, Salem, and Wenham, and DANIEL, of Boston,—who may well have been brothers, although their relationship is a matter of conjecture, nor is it known whence they came. The descendants of John are traced in the following pages. There is a family tradition that the Fairfields are descended from French Huguenots whose name was originally Beauchamp; that a branch of the family was living in France at the time of the massacre of St. Bartholomew's Day, in 1572, and was sufficiently high in court circles to hear of the plot in season to escape to England, where another and elder branch was living at Warwick. Later, on account of religious restraints, some, it is asserted, departed for Ireland, whence John Fairfield came to America, in 1638.

FAIRFIELD ARMS

(from Crozier's General Armory)

Arms—Gules, a lion rampant or.

Crest—On a mount vert, two doves billing proper.

JOHN[1] FAIRFIELD was in Charlestown, Mass., in 1638, says Savage; was granted eighty acres of land in Salem in 1639 (Salem records); was admitted freeman May 14, 1640, (Savage); lived on the boundary line between Salem and Ipswich in 1643 (Salem records); and removed to Wenham, where he died December 22, 1646, (probate records). His will, on file at Salem, dated December 11, 1646, names his wife, Elizabeth, and refers to his three children, but names only two, his sons Walter and Benjamin. There was also a posthumous child.

Children:

I. WALTER[2], b. about 1632; d. July 20, 1723, in ninety-second year (Wenham records)

II. JOHN, b. May, 1639; d. 1672; mentioned as eight years two months old in settlement of estate rendered July 7, 1647; baptized June 27, 1641, (Wenham church records).

III. BENJAMIN, b. Feb.1645, d. in Reading July 14, 1664, (Reading records); mentioned as two years five months old in settlement; baptized April 27, 1646, (Wenham church records).

IV. —, posthumous, b. 1647, but died before July 7; mentioned as five months old in settlement.

The settlement quoted says that the estate was divided into four parts, for the widow and three surviving children. The widow married (2) Peter Palfrey, of Reading, who gave bonds to pay the portions of the three children.

JOHN[2] FAIRFIELD (*John*[1]), son of John and Elizabeth Fairfield, was born, probably in Salem, in May, 1639, and lived in Wenham and Ipswich. He married, March 26, 1666, Sarah Geare (Wenham records), the daughter of William and Tryphena Geare, of Wenham, (Boston Transcript, May 22, 1905). He made no will, but the probate records show that Widow Sarah Fairfield was appointed administratrix of the estate of John Fairfield, of Ipswich, and an inventory was filed November 27, 1672.

Three children are mentioned in that paper:

I. TRYPHENA[3], b. Aug. 2, 1667, (Wenham records); m. Thomas Woodward, of Boston (deed).

II. JOHN, b. probably about 1668.

III. ELIZABETH, possibly m. William Goddard, Oct. 29, 1697, (Boston records).

Mrs. Fairfield married (2) Daniel Kilham April 13, 1673, (Wenham records). She died in Ipswich, January 20, 1715-16, aged seventy years (tombstone).

JOHN[3] FAIRFIELD (*John[2]*, *John[1]*), son of John and Tryphena (Geare) Fairfield, was born probably in Ipswich, about 1668. He was married in Boston, April 18, 1693, by Rev. James Allen, to Elizabeth Badson, (Boston Record Commissioners' Report, vol. 9, p. 209). A deed shows that he was living in Ipswich in January 1690, but December 12, 1692, John and Elizabeth Fairfield (his sister), of Muddy River (Brookline), children and heirs of John Fairfield, late of Ipswich, deceased, sold land in Wenham and Ipswich (Essex deeds). The year following his marriage he was back in Ipswich, as indicated by a deed of John Fairfield and wife, Elizabeth, of Ipswich, February 28, 1693-94, (Essex deeds). March 12, 1693-94, John Fairfield deeded to William Fairfield (his cousin) about sixty acres of upland and meadow in Wenham, saying it formerly belonged to John Fairfield, of Wenham, deceased, (his grandfather), and "from him to my father, John Fairfield of Ipswich, now deceased, and to my uncle, Walter Fairfield of Wenham, said William's father." He acknowledged this deed

November 25, 1703, (Essex deeds). A study and comparison of the town records of Boston, Ipswich, and Wenham shows, by process of elimination, that he was the father of Capt. JOHN FAIRFIELD of Kennebunkport, Me., born before 1700. The names of other children have not been found.

Capt. JOHN[4] FAIRFIELD (John[3], John[2], John[1]), son of John and Elizabeth (Badson) Fairfield, was the first of the name to settle in Kennebunkport, where he was a leading citizen. He was said to have come from Worcester. For a number of years he lived in Wells, as shown by the York County deeds. He was a carpenter. Says Bradbury's History of Kennebunkport: "Mr. Fairfield lived near the mouth of Kennebunk River, probably in the house built by Thomas Perkins in 1733, and was licensed to keep tavern. He afterwards removed to the eastern part of the town, but bought the farm now (1837) belonging to the heirs of William Fairfield in 1764." In the Louisburg expedition of 1745 he was first lieutenant in Capt. John Storer's company (*N. E. Hist. and Gen. Reg.*, vol 22, p. 116). In 1748 he served in Capt. Thomas Perkins's company at Arundel (Mass. Muster Rolls, vol. 92, p. 146, vol. 93, p. 1). In 1757 he was captain of the Arundel company in the First York County Regiment, Sir William Pepperell, colonel, in which company his sons John and Stephen also served. (Muster Rolls, vol. 95, pp. 355, 358).

Capt. Fairfield married (1) Mary, daughter of Rev. Samuel and Tabitha (Littlefield) Emery, of Wells, born December 7, 1699, (Emery Genealogy). Rev. Samuel Emery (1670-1724) was for many years minister in Wells. He was the son of John Emery, Jr., and grandson of John Emery, of Romsey, Hants, England, who came to America in 1635 with his brother Anthony, and settled in Newbury, Mass. (2) After 1750 Mrs. Hannah (Lovet) Stone, widow of Jonathan Stone (History of Kennebunkport), who survived him. He died in 1778. October 22d of that year administration was granted on his estate to his son John "of said Arundel, gentleman," who sold his homestead at auction to Capt. William Fairfield, grandson of the deceased. The inventory of his estate included a negro girl valued at twenty pounds. (York probate records, vol. 13, pp. 122, 148, 162.)

Children by first marriage (History of Kennebunkport, and town records):

    I. JOHN[5], b. 1728 or 1730.

    II. DAUGHTER, m. John Haley.

III. MARY, m. March 26, 1756, Benjamin
Downing, son of Deacon Benjamin
and Elizabeth Downing, b. March
12, 1732; d. Jan. 27, 1797.

IV. STEPHEN, m. Elizabeth Smith and
removed to Wells; he saw service in
the French and Indian Wars, parti-
cipating with Col. Preble's regiment
in the Lake George expedition in
1758 (Mass. Muster Rolls, vol. 96, p.
498), and as sergeant with Col.
Willard's regiment in the expedition to Crown Point in 1759 (Muster
Rolls, vol. 97, p. 327).

V. ELIZABETH, m. Dixey Stone.

JOHN[5] FAIRFIELD   (John[4],   John[3],   John[2],
John[1]),son of Capt. John and Mary (Emery)
Fairfield, was born about 1728 or 1730 in
Kennebunkport, where he resided all his life.
In 1757 he served in the company commanded
by his father in Col. Pepperell's regiment
(Muster Rolls, vol. 95, p. 358), and in 1762 was
ensign in Capt. Thomas Perkins's Arundel
company, Col. Nathaniel Sparhawk's regiment
(Muster Rolls, vol. 99, p. 42). He married
October 17, 1751, Mary Burbank of Bradford,

Mass. (Bradford town records,) born 1733,
died 1825, aged ninety-two (family records).
She was the daughter of Lieut. John and
Priscilla (Major) Burbank, her father having
been a lieutenant in Capt. Thomas Perkins's
company at the taking of Louisburg.

Children, (family and town records):

I. SAMUEL[6], b. Nov. 24, 1752; d. June
14, 1828; m. April 11, 1782, Sarah
Huff, daughter of Charles and
Priscilla (Burbank) Huff.

II. WILLIAM, b. Dec. 26, 1754; d. March
16, 1827; a Revolutionary soldier.

III. SARAH, Feb. 28, 1757; m. Dec. 2,
1779, Israel Whitten.

IV. JOHN, Jan. 3, 1759; d. June 10, 1834;
m. Dec. 30, 1784, Hannah, daughter
of James and Hannah (Merrill)
Burnham; a Revolutionary soldier.

V. STEPHEN, b. Nov. 24, 1762; d. at sea,
unmarried; a Revolutionary soldier;
administration granted on his
estate Nov. 20, 1815; termed in
court paper "late mariner in the
navy in the service of the United
States."

VI. MARY, b. June 28, 1765; d. Sept. 2, 1827; m. Oct. 28, 1784, Robert Towne.

VII. BENJAMIN, b. Jan. 18, 1768; d. at sea.

VIII. ASA, b. March 10, 1771; d. at sea.

IX. MOSES, b. June 18, 1773; lost at sea; m. Nov. 26, 1797, Betsy, daughter of Wheelwright and Phebe (Smith) Stevens.

X. ELIZABETH, b. Sept. 22, 1776; d. July 22, 1798; m. Sept. 14, 1796, Alexander Gould.

Capt. WILLIAM[6] FAIRFIELD (*John[5], John[4], John[3], John[2], John[1]*), son of John and Mary (Burbank) Fairfield, was born in Kennebunkport, Dec. 26, 1754, and died there March 16, 1827. He was a master mariner and made many voyages. In 1777 he enlisted for three years in the Revolutionary army, and served in Capt. Daniel Merrill's company, Col. Samuel Brewer's regiment, and also Capt. Hitchcock's company, Col. Ebenezer Sprout's regiment. His name appears on the Continental army pay accounts for service from February 1, 1777, to February 1, 1780, and he was allowed for travel from his home to Bennington, Vt., the place of rendezvous (Massachusetts Muster Rolls). He married (1) December 27, 1781, Sarah Burnham, daughter of James and Grace (Delzell) Burnham (Bradbury and town records); (2) August 25, 1790, Mary, daughter of David and Elizabeth (Gray) King, of Biddeford, born December 14, 1773, died April 9, 1851, (family records). (See King family.)

Children (family records):

By first marriage:

 I. JAMES[7], b. Dec. 6, 1784; d. July 22, 1820; m. Lois —.

 II. WILLIAM b. Jan. 29, 1786; d. Nov. 7, 1811.

 III. MARY, b. May 17, 1787; d. Aug. 7, 1870; m. John Lord.

 IV. SARAH, b. March 2, 1790; d. young.

By second marriage:

 V. Capt. OLIVER, b. Jan. 1, 1794; d. March 24, 1883; m. (1) Sarah Alden Hayes (1796–1827), his cousin, daughter of Deacon John and Sarah Alden (King) Hayes (see King family); (2) Mrs. Sarah Lord Kimball; (3) Emma Hart; res. Fort Wayne, Ind.

VI. ALEXANDER, b. Aug. 2, 1795; d. Dec. 1, 1872; went to Canada; fourteen children.

VII. Capt. ASA, b. Jan. 28, 1797; d. Oct. 4, 1868; res. Fort Wayne, Ind.

VIII. CYRUS KING, b. March 13, 1799; d. March 23, 1811.

IX. MIRANDA, b. Nov. 5, 1800; d. June 27, 1878.

X. LUCINDA, b. Nov. 20, 1802; d. Dec. 31, 1887.

XI. ELIZA, b. July 15, 1804; April 19, 1806.

XII. JOHN, b. March 4, 1806; d. April 6, 1833.

XIII. JOSEPH, b. Sept. 23, 1807; d. Jan. 30, 1893; unmarried.

XIV. CHARLES, b. Feb. 14, 1809; d. Oct. 26, 1898; res. Fort Wayne, Ind.

XV. JANE, b. May 5, 1811; d. May 12, 1884. m. Nahum Haley, of Kennebunkport.

XVI. WILLIAM, b. May 31, 1813; d. April 26, 1815.

XVII. SARAH, b. Jan. 10, 1816; d. Aug. 5, 1893; m. C. S. Silver; res. Portland, Ore.

XVIII. GEORGE, b. Sept. 2, 1818; d. June 1, 1836.

Capt. Oliver Fairfield and Capt. Asa Fairfield served in the War of 1812, were taken prisoners, and for a time were confined in Dartmoor Prison, England.

LUCINDA[7] FAIRFIELD (*William*[6], *John*[5], *John*[4], *John*[3], *John*[2], *John*[1]), daughter of Capt. William and Mary (King) Fairfield, was born in Kennebunkport November 20, 1802, and died December 31, 1887. She married (1) Aug. 11, 1823, Capt. Isaac Emery, of Kennebunk, son of Isaac and Eunice (Perkins) Emery, who was born July 24, 1795, and died at sea in 1830. He was sixth in descent from Anthony Emery, of Dover and Kittery, who came to this country with his brother John in 1635; and his mother (1761-1834) was the daughter of Eliphalet and Mary (Perkins) Perkins; (2) Clement Perkins, born March 23, 1807, died March 4, 1884.

Children by first marriage:

  I. SUSAN D.[8], b. Oct. 19, 1824; m. Robert W. Towne.

  II. MARY L., b. April 12, 1826; m. Cyrus Fenderson.

  III. EUNICE P., b. April 17, 1828; m. (1) Joseph Wheelwright; (2) H. Smart.

  IV. CHARLES ISAAC, b. Aug. 12, 1830; m. April 25, 1854, Sarah Perkins.

(For children by second marriage, see Clement Perkins.)

Descent Of Governor John Fairfield, Of Maine

John[1], of Salem and Wenham, d. Dec. 22, 1646; m. Elizabeth —.

Walter[2], b. 1632; d. in Wenham, July 20, 1723; m. Sarah Skipper.

William[3], b. in Reading, Oct. 14, 1662; d. in Wenham, Dec. 18, 1742; m. Esther —; representative from Wenham to General Court for many years; speaker, 1741.

William[4], b. in Wenham, 1693, d. in Boston, May 13, 1770; m. (2) Elizabeth White.

Rev. John[5], b. in Boston, Dec. 26, 1737; d. in Saco, Me., Dec. 16, 1819; m. Mary (Goodwin) Cotts; for many years minister at Saco.

Ichabod[6], b. in Saco, May 1, 1763; d. in Saco, March 19, 1824; m. Sarah (Nason) Scammon.

Gov. John[7], b. in Saco, Jan. 30, 1797; d. in Washington, Dec. 24, 1847; m. Anne Paine Thornton; member of Congress, 1835–39; governor of Maine, 1839–40, 1842–43; United States senator, 1843–47.

There lived in West Newton, Mass., within the memory of living men, an old lady by the name of Hoppin, who said she was a servant in the family of Rev. John Fairfield when she was sixteen years old, and once, while riding with her in his chaise to Kennebunkport, he told her that he was related to the Fairfields of that town. In the York Institute, Saco, is the diary of Parson Fairfield, wherein he says, June 16, 1773, "Capt. John Fairfield (of Kennebunkport) lodged here."

KING FAMILY

KING FAMILY

The accounts of the first American ancestor of the King families of Scarboro and Saco, Maine, are meager. Dr. Charles R. King, in The Life and Correspondence of Rufus King, says:

1. "JOHN[1] KING, who came to America from Kent, England, soon after the year 1700, settled in Boston, and in 1714 married Sarah Allen, by whom he had a son, who died in infancy. Upon her death he married Mary Stowell, daughter of Benjamin Stowell, of Newton, Mass., in 1718, and by her had several children, of whom Richard, the eldest, was born in Boston in 1718."

The marriage intentions of John King, of Boston, and Mary Stowell, of Newton, April 2, 1718, appear on the Boston records (Record Commissioners' Report, vol. 28, p. 97).

The following births are also recorded:

Mary, daughter of John and Mary King, June 8, 1719, (vol. 24, p. 137).

Sarah, daughter of John and Mary King, February 27, 1720, (vol. 24, p. 148).

No record of other births is to be found. Southgate, in his History of Scarboro, to which town Richard King removed, states that Richard had three brothers,—David, Josiah, and William,—of whom David was "sometime a merchant in Saco," and William a sea captain. In the *Maine Historical and Genealogical Recorder* (vol. 1) a memorandum is presented, made from a statement of a granddaughter of Richard King, that he had a brother (David) and two sisters living in Saco. "The sisters were named Grandy and Kneeland, both widows, and always known as the 'English ladies,' because of their stately bearing, and from having 'come from England.'" The marriages of the two sisters are recorded in Boston:

Dec. 9, 1735, John Kneeland and Mehitable King (vol. 28, p. 182).

June 25, 1738, Joseph Grandy and Mary King (vol. 28, p. 206).

Widow Kneeland died May 15, 1810, (Saco Records). If Richard King was born in 1718, Mary in 1719, and Sarah in 1720, Mehitable could not have been born before 1721, and was therefore only fourteen years of age when she married Mr. Kneeland. This would have made her eighty-nine years of age at the time of her death.

Recapitulation of children of John and Mary (Stowell) King:

2. I. RICHARD², b. 1718; d. March 17, 1775.

II. MARY, b. June 8, 1719; m. Joseph Grandy.

III. SARAH, b. Feb. 27, 1720.

IV. MEHITABLE, b. prob. 1721; m. John Kneeland; d. May 15, 1810.

3. V. DAVID, b. Aug. 21, 1726, (family records); d. March 11, 1807, (Saco Records).

VI. JOSIAH.

VII. WILLIAM.

2. RICHARD² KING (*John¹*), son of John and Mary (Stowell) King, was born in Boston in 1718, and died in Scarboro, Maine, March 17, 1775. Says Dr. Charles R. King: "In 1740 he settled in Watertown, Mass., in prosperous business as a trader and factor for Ebenezer Thornton, one of the principal merchants in Boston, for whom he purchased and prepared large quantities of timber. It is probable that in the prosecution of the timber business he visited Scarboro, for in 1744 he was at that place, though he did not remain there. In the spring of 1745, on the invitation of Gov. Shirley, he

took part as a commissary of subsistence, with the rank of captain, in the famous expedition against Cape Breton. He sailed with the expedition for Louisburg, and was present at the capture of that fortress. On his return he sold his properties in Watertown and removed permanently to Scarboro until his death, on March 17, 1775. He was both a farmer and a merchant, and in each capacity was so successful as to become the owner of three thousand acres of land, and to be the largest exporter of lumber from Maine. For the last twenty years of his life he was the foremost man in Scarboro. ... A fire which occurred a few years before his death destroyed nearly all his papers, and probably what family records he had."

He was twice married: (1) November 20, 1753, to Isabella Bragdon, of York, born April 8, 1731, died October 19, 1759, daughter of Samuel and Tabitha (Banks) Bragdon, of York; her sister, Tabitha, born December 1, 1723, married Stephen Longfellow, great grandfather of the poet Longfellow. (2) January 31, 1762, to his first wife's cousin, Mary Black, daughter of Samuel and Isabella (Bragdon) Black, of York, born October 8, 1736, died May 19, 1816. (From *Maine Historical and Genealogical Recorder*, vol. 1, which also gives data of children, below.)

Children:

By first marriage:

4. I. RUFUS[3], b. March 24, 1755; d. April 29, 1827.

II. MARY, 1757; d. March 30, 1824; m. June 23, 1773; Dr. Robert Southgate, of Scarboro.

III. PAULINA, b. 1759; m. April 13, 1777; Aaron Porter of Portland; among her descendants was Rev. Dr. Egbert C. Smyth, president of Andover Theological Seminary.

By second marriage:

5. IV. RICHARD, b. Dec. 22, 1762; d. Oct. 27, 1830.

V. ISABELLA, b. Sept. 8, 1764; d. Sept. 12, 1770.

VI. DORCAS, b. May 20, 1766; m. Dec 28, 1786, Joseph Leland.

6. VII. WILLIAM, b. Feb. 9, 1768; d. June 17, 1852.

VIII. ELIZABETH, b. Jan. 7, 1770; m. Benjamin Jones Porter.

7. IX. CYRUS, b. Sept. 6, 1772; d. April 25, 1817.

3. DAVID[2] KING (*John[1]*), son of John and
Mary (Stowell) King, was born, probably in
Boston, August 1, 1726, according to the
family records, and died in Buxton, Me., near
the Saco line, March 11, 1807, (Saco Records).
In 1746 he was a witness to a deed by which
his brother Richard, of Boston, conveyed to
Jonas Cooledge, of Boston, land in Watertown
(Middlesex deeds, vol. 45, pp. 96, 517). Mr.
King was for many years a leading merchant
of Saco, Me., to which town he removed,
probably about 1760. A deed of April 21, 1761,
shows a purchase of land by him from James
Miller, on Saco River (York deeds, vol. 36, p.
248). Folsom's History of Saco and Biddeford
(p. 259) includes David King "among the first
merchants or traders of whom we have an
account on the east side of the river." He
traded a short time near the head of one of Sir
William Pepperell's wharves, but soon after his
marriage in 1762 removed to the west side of the
river. March 13, 1777, John Gray, of Biddeford,
deeded to Elizabeth King, wife of David King,
of Biddeford, one hundred and fifty acres of
land in Pepperellboro (Saco; York deeds, vol.
46, p. 16). Mr. King was married by Rev. Moses
Morrill, March 14, 1762, to Elizabeth Gray, of
Biddeford (Biddeford records). She was the
daughter of John Gray. February 8, 1795,

Josiah King, of Colbrook, Grafton County, N. H., in a deed to John Hayes, mentions his mother, Elizabeth King, and her father, John Gray, of Biddeford, deceased. (York deeds, vol. 58, p. 41) Mrs. King was born August, 1745; died March 17, 1777, (family records). Mr. King served in the Revolutionary War in 1775, as sergeant in Captain Benjamin Hooper's company, raised for seacoast defense and stationed at Biddeford; and his name also appears on a list of men belonging to Capt. Hooper's company (Buxton) January, 1782, (Mass. Muster Rolls). Mr. King lived to be nearly eighty-one years of age, and in his last days resided with his daughter, Mrs. Hayes, in Buxton, adjoining Saco, where he died.

Children (family records):

I. JOHN[3], b. Nov. 30, 1762; d. Jan. 16, 1853.

II. DAVID, b. Jan. 5, 1765; d. Dec 1776.

III. WILLIAM, b. Nov. 12, 1766; d. Dec. 31, 1769.

IV. JOSIAH, b. Jan. 12, 1769; removed to New Hampshire.

V. SARAH ALDEN, b. April 23, 1771; m. Deacon John Hayes, of Saco; five children (see Fairfield family).

VI. MARY, b. Dec. 14, 1773; m. Capt. William Fairfield, of Kennebunkport; d. April 9, 1851, (see Fairfield family).

VII. WILLIAM, b. May 17, 1776.

4. Hon. RUFUS[3] KING (*Richard*[2], *John*[1]), son of Richard and Isabella (Bragdon) King, was born in Scarboro, March 24, 1755, and died in New York, April 29, 1829. He was a member of Congress from Massachusetts, United States Senator from New York, and United States minister to London. Married, March 30, 1786, Mary, daughter of Hon. John Alsop, born October 17, 1769.

Children:

I. JOHN ALSOP[4], b. Jan. 3, 1788; d. July 8, 1867; governor of New York; member of Congress from New York; seven children.

II. CHARLES, b. March 16, 1789; d. 1867; president of Columbia College; fourteen children; a grandson is General Charles[6] King, U. S. A., the well-known novelist.

III. JAMES GORE, b. May 8, 1791; prominent banker; member of Congress from New Jersey; ten children.

IV. HENRY, died young.

V. EDWARD, b. March 13, 1799; d. in Cincinnati, 1831; president Ohio State Senate; two children.

VI. FREDERICK GORE, b. Feb. 6, 1802; no children.

VII. CAROLINE, b. Nov. 10, 1813; d. young.

5. RICHARD³ KING (*Richard²*, *John¹*), son of Richard and Mary (Black) King, was born in Scarboro, December 22, 1762, and died in Saco, October 27, 1830. He married, January 14, 1790, Hannah Larrabee. His descendants resided in Saco.
Children:

I. CYRUS⁴, b. May 4, 1790.

II. MARY, b. 1791.

III. WILLIAM, b. 1793.

IV. ELIZA, b. 1796.

(Possibly others.)

6. Hon. WILLIAM³ KING (*Richard²*, *John¹*), son of Richard and Mary (Black) King, was born in Scarboro, Feb 9, 1768, and died in Bath, Me., June 17, 1852. He settled in Bath, where he became one of the largest ship-owners in the United States. He was president of the

Maine constitutional convention in 1820; first governor of Maine (1820-1821); United States commissioner of Spanish claims (1821-24); collector of customs at Bath (1831-34); and for many years a trustee of both Bowdoin and Colby Colleges. He married (1800) Ann Nesbeth, daughter of Major Phoenix and Elizabeth Frazier, of Boston, who was born in 1782, and died in Portland, July 4, 1857.

Children:

    I. MARY ELIZABETH[4], b. Sept. 28, 1817; d. unmarried, 1847.

   II. CYRUS WILLIAM, b. Dec. 25, 1819; d. —; m. Sarah Oakman, daughter of Capt. James and Jane (Randall) Jameson, Oct. 19, 1853; children— Dr. William, b. July 18, 1856, grad. Bowdoin College, 1881; Ann Nesbeth Frazier, b. Jan. 31, 1860.

7. Hon. CYRUS[3] KING (*Richard[2], John[1]*), son of Richard and Mary (Black) King, was born in Scarboro, Sept. 6, 1772, and died in Saco, April 25, 1817. An eminent lawyer and member of Congress from Maine. Married, October, 1797, Hannah, daughter of Capt. Seth and Olive (Jordan) Storer.

Children:

I. MARY CAROLINE[4], b. Jan. 27, 1799; d. Jan. 22, 1867; m. Rev. Benjamin Hale.

II. ANN FRAZIER, b. Dec. 20, 1800; m. Edmund Theodore Bridge.

III. OLIVE STORER, b. Dec. 15, 1802; m. Lauriston Ward.

IV. WILLIAM RUFUS, b. Nov. 16, 1804; d. unmarried, July, 1836; lawyer.

V. ELIZABETH PORTER, b. Feb. 17, 1807; d. unmarried, Oct. 30, 1869.

VI. HANNAH SAPHIRE, b. Feb. 7, 1815; d. Nov. 6, 1880; m. R. H. Haywood, of Buffalo, N. Y.

(Foregoing data regarding children of Richard[2] King mainly from *Maine Genealogical and Historical Recorder*, vol. 1.)

KING ARMS

(from Matthews' American Armory and Blue Book)
Arms—Sable, a lion rampant gardant ermine, between three crosses pattee fitchee at the foot or.
Crest—A lion's gamb erect and erased sable, holding a cross pattee fitchee or.
Motto—"Recte et suaviter."